Heike Gross

Beware Poison!

A horse-owner's guide to harmful
and indigestible plants

CADMOS

Contents

Imprint

Copyright © 2005 by Cadmos Verlag GmbH,
Brunsbek.
Translated by Nigel Suffield-Jones MA
(Cantab), Dip Ed, MITI.
Project Management: The Editmaster Co Ltd,
Northampton.
Layout and design: Ravenstein, Verden.
Photography: Reinhardt Tierfoto, Peter Prohnt
Printing: Rasch, Bramsche.

All rights reserved. This publication
may only be reproduced or stored in a
retrieval system with the prior written
permission of the publisher.
Printed in Germany.

ISBN 3-86127-950-9

In the course of domestication, many horses have lost the natural instinct which keeps them from eating poisonous plants. Thus pasture used by horses must be regularly checked for poisonous plants.

Important things to know about poisonous plants

In woods and open fields, meadows and pasture there are quite a number of plants, shrubs, bushes and trees which are highly poisonous to horses. Unfortunately, many riders often know very little about the appearance of poisonous plants, and sometimes do not recognise in time the danger to their horses of poisoning from plants. In riding schools and on riding courses, far too little attention is given to the subject of poisonous plants.

Poisoning in horses is always linked to mild to severe health problems, and in very serious cases can even lead to death. Because of their anatomical peculiarities, horses cannot vomit, and it is very difficult for them to eliminate poisonous substances from their bodies. Veterinary treatment therefore mainly extends to treatment of the symptoms of poisoning.

This book is for all horse owners, stable hands and riding establishments that want to avoid poisoning or sickness in their horses and ponies from poisonous plants, or from bad and decomposing food.

The most dangerous plants are all illustrated, and this book describes the health problems that can arise for horses, should they eat poisonous plants or unsuitable food.

The reader should thus be helped to avoid cases of poisoning from plants. If, however, poisoning from plants or food does occur, the reader should be able to make an evaluation of the extent of poisoning, and a better recognition of the dangerous effects. In responsible horse management, the health and well-being of the horse are always top priorities, and this also includes a knowledge of poisonous plants from which the horse must be protected.

The poisonous plants presented here are listed according to the degree of severity of their toxic effects, i.e.:

- fatal poisoning
- severe poisoning
- mild poisoning
- mild gastritis.

Further dangers of poisoning resulting from food unsuitable for horses are also indicated.

Please note:

The list of poisonous plants presented in this book makes no claim to completeness

How can poisoning be avoided in horse management?

- **Never** tie up horses to hedges or trees, or let them browse on them.
- **Never** let horses loose on unknown pasture, or let them graze on it.
- **Always** call the vet on the slightest suspicion of poisoning.
- **Never** attempt to treat a case of poisoning yourself.

What are the signs of poisoning in a horse?

The recognisable signs of poisoning after eating harmful plants manifest themselves in the most varied ways and after different periods of time, as individual plants contain poisons of varying strength. Most symptoms are visible in cramp-like attacks of colic, scouring, profuse sweating, staggering and changes in behaviour. The poison from a plant can produce an effect on a horse very quickly, but the symptoms of poisoning can also appear after some hours or days.

What should be done if poisoning occurs?

If there is a suspicion of poisoning, the vet must be informed at once. He should be notified on the telephone of the nature of the poison, so that he can obtain the appropriate medication or discuss immediate treatment in detail on the spot. Home-made remedies should never be administered.

Tip

Before calling the vet, the following details should be noted and stated on the telephone:
- *When was the poisonous plant eaten?*
- *What was eaten (for example, which poisonous plant)?*
- *How much was eaten?*
- *What behavioural peculiarities is the horse showing?*
- *How big and how old is the horse?*
- *In what condition is the horse?*
- *Leave a telephone number for a return call if necessary*

The rider should if possible keep a piece of the eaten plant, if no one present is able to identify the plant precisely. In that way, targeted treatment can be instigated against the poison.

Horses which are suspected poisoning victims must be prevented from eating any more food, but water should be available in sufficient quantities. If the horse shows severe loss of balance, it should be put in a spacious loose box with deep straw, so that the horse is not in danger of damaging itself if it falls over.

Uncontrolled browsing on bushes and twigs can have severe consequences for a horse's health.

Useful information on the eating habits of horses

In their daily forays on the vast steppes, wild horses look for food on pasture, forest edges and the banks of streams. They unerringly choose only healthy and edible plants, leaving the poisonous ones alone. Through instincts developed over thousands of years, they know precisely which grasses and plants they can eat, and which ones they must avoid at all costs. Poisoning or malfunction of their digestive system is extremely unlikely, due to this basic instinct in wild horses. Using their natural instinct, sick horses in the wild look for special herbs with the appropriate properties

to contribute to the healing of their ailment. This ability to distinguish between edible, inedible and poisonous plants and bushes has been lost by many horses in the course of their evolution from wild to domestic horses.

However, specialist literature still glibly advances the view that "horses instinctively avoid all poisonous plants". Particularly with plants that are atypical of pasture, for example exotic ornamental trees or garden plants, as occur overwhelmingly in built-up areas, horses do not distinguish between poisonous and harmless plants. Those horses which are kept purely in a loose box regime will eat everything they are offered whilst out on a hack, as they will crave fresh green matter of any sort, whether poisonous or not.

Some of the most poisonous plants taste so bitter that horses fortunately avoid them after the first bite. However, even the smallest quantities of these highly poisonous leaves can lead to the death of the animal. Pasture must be checked regularly and carefully for poisonous plant growth. If poisonous plants are present, they must be dug up completely, including the root ball. Some plants retain their poisonous properties even in the dried state or after lengthy storage, and can even cause health hazards in winter hay used as fodder.

The horse owner bears the considerable responsibility of protecting his horse from eating harmful plants and food. Unfortunately it happens again and again that vets are called to emergencies where poisoning is the root cause, and, depending on the nature and severity of the poisoning, saving the horse is often no longer possible.

However, not all inedible plants immediately result in death. Some cause severe colic, with later serious consequences for the horse, and others simply lead to mild illness.

Food suitable for horses

Hay, oats and straw are the most well-known basic food for horses. They are the most frequently used, and obviously every horse owner is familiar with them. A wide range of supplements have been added in recent years, put together to satisfy the most varied needs of horse nutrition. When using these compounds the horse owner can be certain of only offering the horse edible food, provided that the hay, straw and corn are of good quality and free of mould. With power feed mixtures, care must be taken not to pass the use-by date.

Besides this multiplicity of feeds there are ready-made herb mixtures for the relief of sickness or lameness and for improving the general health of a horse.

Can herbs in every form be used entirely safely?

Many horse owners buy herb mixtures for their horse from specialist dealers, and the manufacturer will have made certain that these ready-made mixtures are safe. They contain no plants with a toxic effect, or, in cases where such plants are included for specific healing properties, only in quite small, digestible quantities.

Plants gathered for one's own mixture are only to be fed safely to the horse if the owner is really knowledgeable about the individual substances in the medicinal plants and the right quantity to administer. This implies a very extensive knowledge of herbs and medicinal plants. In cases of doubt or insufficient knowledge it is always better only to use ready-made mixtures from a specialist dealer.

Plants with a deadly effect

Ornamental gardens, woods, woodland edges and stream banks harbour many deadly plants among their grasses and shrubs. So as not to run even the slightest risk of poisoning from plants, horses basically should not be allowed to eat any green matter while out riding. This requires persistent training by the rider, but will certainly protect the horse from the risk of a severe or even fatal illness.

The danger of poisoning is always there when owners offer their horses titbits in the form of flowers, grasses or twigs that they themselves have picked, not knowing their chemical content or potential harmful effects.

Below is a list of those plants whose poisonous active ingredients can lead to the death of a horse within a few hours:

Cuckoo Pint, Lords and Ladies
(Arum maculatum)

Cuckoo Pint grows especially in woodland edges, and in deciduous and mixed woodland. Besides aroin, it also contains small amounts of hydrogen cyanide. The whole plant is highly poisonous. It produces swellings of the mucous membranes and scouring, along with intestinal bleeding and cessation of peristalsis (peristaltic motion).

Giant Hogweed
(Heracleum mantegazzianum)

This imposing plant can reach a height of up to 3.50 metres and is easily recognised. All parts of the plant, but especially the juice, are very poisonous. Contact with the skin of the rider or the coat of the horse in conditions of sunlight can lead to swellings and blistering, similar to burning. Therefore make sure to avoid touching this plant on a ride. Eating this plant leads to life-threatening irritations of the mucous membranes.

Henbane (Hyoscyamus niger)

The black, very unpleasant smelling henbane grows on the sides of tracks and roads. All parts of the plant are highly poisonous due to the alkaloid content, and can lead to the death of the horse within a few hours even after only a small amount has been eaten. Poisoning is shown by accelerated heartbeat, tying-up of the muscles, paralysis and severe colic.

Box *(Buxus sempervirens)*

Box also is one of the plants with fatal consequences, 750 grams of the small leaves being enough to poison a horse. When landscaping riding establishments, the choice of plants and shrubs must make reference to their toxicity. Even so, there are remarkably frequent cases of stables on whose land grow evergreen and highly poisonous plants like yew and box. At such establishments the horse owner must watch his horse very carefully. Box produces severe colic and central nervous paralysis, with death arising from cardiac and respiratory arrest.

Beechnut

In the autumn beechnuts are frequent in the woods, but horses must be prevented from eating them, as one kilogram of beechnuts contains a dose of tannic acid that is dangerous for horses.

Monkshood *(Aconitum napellus)*

Monkshood is one of the most poisonous plants in Europe. All parts of the plant are highly poisonous, but particularly the roots and seed, which contain the deadly poison aconitin. With acute poisoning death occurs after one to three hours. The effects are severe colic, scouring and inflammation of the kidneys leading to kidney failure.

Yew *(Taxus baccata)*

Yew is one of the most deadly poisonous plants for horses. Just a few twigs (100 grams of needles) are sufficient to poison a horse. The dangerous aspect of a yew is that it can easily be confused with the harmless pine and spruce. It can in fact be distinguished by the structure of its needles: yew needles are very soft and flat, and are shiny on the top. The yew also has red fruits.

Yew contains the poisons taxine, formic acid and hydrocyanic acid in high dosages. These plant poisons first of all produce states of excitement, with accelerated pulse rate, after which follows paralysis of the respiratory muscles. Death occurs very suddenly from heart failure. Saving the horse is only possible in rare cases with immediate veterinary assistance.

Brugmansia *(Datura suaveolens)*

All parts of the brugmansia are poisonous, as it belongs to the nightshades. Overwhelmingly, these plants are found in ornamental and domestic gardens. Just small quantities produce severe colic, and there is a significant danger of death for the horse.

11

Foxglove *(Digitalis purpurea)*

This biennial, very bitter-tasting herb grows in light woodland and is also cultivated as an ornamental plant. The very strong poison from the red flower is retained in the heart, and 100 grams of fresh leaves can kill a horse. In its dried state, moreover, this plant is also highly poisonous in hay. Poisoning by foxgloves causes sweating, cardiac paralysis and circulatory disorders.

Runner Beans, Green Beans *(Phaseolus coccineus)*

The raw beans and particularly the seeds are very poisonous. Some hours after eating them, the symptoms are bloody scouring, severe colic and a raised pulse rate. Danger from eating this vegetable arises if pasture directly borders on kitchen gardens, and the animals can reach the bean plants over the fence.

Laburnum *(Laburnum anagyroides)*

Laburnum is frequently found as an ornamental shrub in gardens in built-up areas. Just 200 grams of the seed contain enough poison to kill a horse. Poisoning due to laburnum is evident in increased salivation, increased respiratory rate, tying-up of the muscles and scouring. Death occurs from paralysis of the respiratory muscles and respiratory arrest.

Autumn Crocus *(Colchicum autumnale)*

Autumn crocus is a very poisonous cormous plant, and popularly has the reputation of being a suicide plant. It grows on damp ground and in woodland clearings. It causes severe sweating, tying-up of the muscles and colic with bloody scouring. Death occurs from paralysis of the respiratory muscles and respiratory arrest.

Privet *(Liguster vulgare)*

If a horse eats just 100 grams of privet, it is sufficient to kill it. Privet is a widely used hedging plant, particularly in built-up areas with detached family houses and ornamental gardens.

Oleander *(Nerium oleander)*

As few as 10 leaves of oleander can be sufficient to kill a horse. The poison, which is most strongly concentrated in the evergreen leaves, produces scouring and colic initially. However, as there are many other possible causes of these symptoms, this poisoning is extremely pernicious, and difficult to recognise. The horse finally dies from cardiac arrest and paralysis of the respiratory muscles.

Mezereon *(Daphne mezereum)*

Mezereon grows on dry areas and heathland. Just 30 grams of this plant can be fatal for horses, as all parts of the plant contain the sharp-tasting poison mezerin. It causes severe swelling of the mucous membranes in the mouth, and inflammation of the gut.

Greater Celandine *(Chelidonium majus)*

Greater celandine is a very undemanding plant, found under walls and hedges, and on waste ground, especially on calcareous soil. The whole plant, but especially the latex, is highly poisonous. Accelerated breathing and bloody scouring are the most common effects.

Thornapple *(Datura stramonium)*

The strongly alkaline seeds are extremely poisonous, and all other parts of the plant are very poisonous. If the horse has eaten just a few grams of this plant, heavy sweating is followed by a paralysis of the central nervous system, which in its advanced state severely weakens the horse and brings on staggering. The poisoning can result in fatal respiratory arrest.

Deadly Nightshade *(Atropa belladonna)*

The leaves and seed of the deadly nightshade are highly poisonous, and just 125 grams of the seed contain a quantity of poison that is fatal for a horse. The plant mainly contains atropine, which produces an accelerated pulse, heavy sweating and intestinal disorders.

Cowbane *(Cicuta virosa)*

This strongly poisonous plant grows on the banks of streams, in marshy areas and around the edges of ponds. It has an unpleasant smell and the stalk is filled with a yellow juice which is very poisonous. Just 10 grams is a fatal dosage for horses. Poisoning is visible in loss of balance, with death occurring through paralysis of the respiratory muscles.

Plants which cause severe poisoning

The following plants are very poisonous, and cause the most serious symptoms of poisoning. Through timely veterinary assistance it is usually possible to avert the death of the horse, or severe illnesses with damaging consequences for overall health.

Some of these plants are again found predominantly in ornamental gardens and parkland, and for this reason horses out riding basically should be prevented from nibbling and eating, for their own protection.

If pasture or paddocks are in the immediate vicinity of houses and ornamental gardens, a second fence should be installed to create a safety zone from the woody plants and shrubs growing there. Immediate neighbours must be most strongly requested not to put garden refuse in the pasture. Those living nearby no doubt only mean to be kind to the horses when they tip their garden refuse or grass cuttings on the pasture. However, freshly mown grass cuttings produce serious colic.

Unfortunately many horses have died in this way. Foals particularly are very inquisitive, and enjoy nibbling at or actually eating everything they do not know. They must therefore be especially protected from unfamiliar green matter in their meadows. Abnormal behaviour of horses at pasture, like sweating, foaming from the mouth and the nostrils, salivation, shortness of breath, sensitivity to the touch, loss of balance and shivering must not be ignored, as they may well be the first indications of poisoning.

In horses at pasture, illnesses can be caused not only by poisonous plants, but also by freshly fertilised meadows and pesticides. These can produce the severest nitrate or heavy metal poisoning.

If one or even several horses in a pasture display unusual behaviour or indications of the symptoms mentioned above, the vet should be notified in every case as quickly as possible, to check their state of health.

Even in the dried state, some poisonous plants still retain their active ingredients, and are contained in hay, giving rise to colic and other clinical signs. For this reason the hay crop should only be taken from "clean" fields which are free from poisonous plants. It is advisable not to mow too close to bordering woodland edges, as ferns, henbane and foxgloves frequently thrive there, and in no circumstances should come into the hay crop.

Yellow Pheasant's-eye *(Adonis vernalis)*

Yellow pheasant's-eye grows on calcareous, dry ground. Eating it causes shortness of breath, swellings of the mucous membranes, scouring and loss of balance.

Christmas Rose *(Helleborus niger)*

The Christmas rose is less often encountered, and so the risk that horses will eat it is small. It only grows on humus-rich ground. All parts of the plant are poisonous, causing states of excitement and paralysis of the central nervous system.

Ivy *(Hedera helix)*

Large quantities of ivy lead to severe colic, as it contains poisonous saponins. One should therefore be wary of pasture which borders house walls covered in ivy.

Ferns
(Pteridium aquilinum, Dryopteris filix mas)

Bracken and male ferns grow in woodland edges and clearings. They are the most dangerous representatives of this genus of plants. Skittishness, tying-up of the muscles and bloody scouring are the consequences of poisoning by ferns. These signs of illness often do not occur directly after ingestion, but only some days later, so that the connection between the illness and eating fern frequently remains unnoticed. If the horse eats a large quantity of fern over a longer period (for example, on being put out to pasture near woodland), these symptoms can become more severe to the extent that, without veterinary assistance, they lead to the death of the horse.

Broom *(Cytisus scoparius)*

Broom is frequently used as an ornamental plant in hedges. It grows wild on the edge of woodland and in clearings, as well as on heathland. The whole plant is poisonous, producing a raised pulse rate and paralysis of the respiratory tract, with death resulting from asphyxiation.

Potatoes (Solanum tuberosum)
Raw potatoes and especially the foliage of the plant cannot be tolerated at all by horses, and must never be any part of their food. Eating them causes irritation of the gut, tying-up of the muscles, scouring and severe colic as well as damage to the blood cells.

Common Ragwort
(Senecio jacobaea)

Common ragwort often grows on embankments, the sides of tracks and the edges of woodland. The herb contains alkaloids, and also remains poisonous in its dried state, thus presenting a risk in hay. The symptoms of ragwort poisoning are constipation, loss of appetite and a swaying gait. Consumed in significant quantities, it can lead to liver damage. Saving the horse is possible with timely veterinary assistance.

Thuja, Cypress Spurge
(Euphorbia cyparissias)

This very frequently grown ornamental shrub, often used as a hedge in built-up areas, contains the poisonous euphorbon and additional volatile oils in its sap. Unfortunately, riders mostly consider this plant to be like the harmless pines or spruces, and are not concerned if their horses eat it. The poisonous substances produce severe irritation of the mucous membranes and colic. In a more advanced state it leads to liver damage, which if untreated can cause death.

Lupin *(Lupinus)*

The lupin frequently grows in calcium deficient soils on embankments or field edges. It is very unhealthy for horses because of its high albumen content. The main concentration of the poisonous substances is contained in the seeds. It contains alkaloids, causing states of excitement, tying-up of the muscles, liver damage and laminitis.

Lily of the Valley *(Convallaria majalis)*

The lily of the valley grows in shady woodland and gardens, and belongs to the lily family. Its taste is sharp, bitter and repulsive. All parts of the plant are poisonous, and with excessive consumption lead to scouring, stupefaction and circulatory collapse.

Black Nightshade *(Solanum nigrum)*

Black nightshade grows on the sides of tracks, rubbish dumps and in fields of weeds, and is not fussy about soil. All parts of the plant are poisonous, its alkaloids causing weakness and listlessness, and even collapse.

Wild Daffodil
(Narcissus pseudonarcissus)

The wild daffodil, also known as the Lent lily, on its own only represents a small danger to the health of the horse. However, if the bulb is eaten with it, this can lead to severe colic.

Spindle-tree
(Euonymus europaeus)

The spindle-tree grows in woods and on the sides of tracks. The seed of this shrub in particular contains a very poisonous and bitter constituent. Depending on the quantity eaten, horses suffer from circulatory disorders, intestinal problems and scouring.

Rhododendron *(Rhododendron)*

All species of this ornamental plant cause irritation of the mucous membranes, bloody scouring and severe colic.

False Acacia *(Robinia pseudoacacia)*

Robinia is frequently confused with acacia, and so is known under the name "false acacia". Poisoning caused by robinia twigs starts with colic, and later cardiac insufficiency and brain damage. The poisonous agent is the alkaloid-like and albumen-like robin, as well as tannins and volatile oils. The highly poisonous robin resides especially in the bark, less so in the leaves and seeds. These poisons cause colic, and there is a noticeable decrease in the volume of droppings. Subsequently, there is intestinal bleeding and paralysis of the large intestine, which are brought on by disorders of the central nervous system.

Holly *(Ilex aquifolium)*

Holly has very hard, almost leathery leaves with spiny margins. For this reason horses very seldom eat this plant, and cases of serious poisoning are rare.

Plants which induce mild poisoning

In the plant world there are also some plants and shrubs which are merely slightly poisonous, their consumption "only" causing moderate gastritis and general indisposition.

Even if no life-threatening poisoning occurs on these occasions, care must be taken that horses have no access to these plants. Determining the cause of poisoning becomes more difficult if various riders have been with a horse across open country, and cannot state precisely when and where the horse has eaten which plants or shrubs.

Barberry (Berberis vulgaris)

Barberry belongs to the sea buckthorn family, and grows in woodland edges and light mixed woods on calcareous soil. The most poisonous part of the plant is the bark of the root, followed by the bark of the stem. Buds, the flesh of the fruit and the seeds are generally free of alkaloid. Only in a higher dosage can mild poisoning occur, which, however, is not life-threatening. Scouring and colic can occur.

Wood Anemone, Wind Flower
(Anemone nemerosa)

The wood anemone belongs to the buttercup family, and all parts of the plant are slightly poisonous, due to the poison anemonin. It mostly grows in meadows, or near bushes. If horses eat this plant, irritation of the mucous membranes of the mouth and throat can occur, and scouring is also possible.

Meadow Buttercup (Ranunculus acris)

All parts of the meadow buttercup are poisonous. It grows in meadows, as well as on the edges of roads and tracks. It can frequently be found in pasture, but horses generally nibble away the grass around the plant, leaving the stalks alone. Only very hungry horses in their craving inadvertently eat the meadow buttercup, which can cause poisoning with swellings of the mucous membranes, scouring, irritation and inflammation of the intestinal area, and paralysis of the respiratory tract. In the dried state the meadow buttercup loses its toxicity, and can be consumed in hay without cause for concern.

Mountain Ash, Rowan *(Sorbus aucuparia)*

The mountain ash loves damp, acid soil, and occurs in almost all woodland areas. The plant is mildly poisonous, and causes mild gastritis if large quantities are eaten.

Common Poppy *(Papaver rhoeas)*

The common poppy grows in nutrient rich, loamy soils on field boundaries. Particularly the latex in the plant contains poisonous alkaloids. Gastritis with colic and scouring can occur.

Not all kinds of vegetables are suitable for feeding to horses. In no circumstances should cabbages, potatoes, onions or tomatoes be used as fodder.

Vegetables which must not be used as fodder

Not all kinds of vegetables are suitable food for horses. The following are completely unsuitable, and must be avoided in all circumstances:

Raw potatoes and potato shoots produce intestinal irritation, as well as tying-up of the muscles and colic, with progressive damage to blood cells, and must not feature in any feeding schedule for horses.

Onions, consumed over a long period, cause anaemia (the red corpuscles are damaged), jaundice and discoloration of the urine.

Cabbage plants lead to flatulence and induce colic.

Tomatoes are members of the nightshade family, and are harmful for horses.

Bean seeds contain dangerous toxins, and cause severe colic with destruction of the mucous membranes of the gut.

Stone fruit like plums, peaches, damsons and cherries are very indigestible for horses, and cause constipation with severe attacks of colic.

No kinds of stone fruit, like the blue and yellow plums shown here, may be fed
to horses, as the stones are very difficult to digest, and can cause colic.

Fungi are very seldom eaten by horses, even when they do grow here and there on pasture. Most kinds of fungi cause mild indisposition, only a few kinds being extremely poisonous.

Poisonous fungi

Only seldom do horses eat fungi. Most poisonous fungi do not grow in the immediate vicinity of horse pasture, where occasionally the harmless field mushroom can be found.

As horse and rider generally follow marked woodland tracks on a ride, they seldom go near poisonous fungi, which mostly grow deep in the underwood. If, unexpectedly, a horse does happen to have eaten fungi, the behaviour of the animal should be watched closely for a few hours. Only a few kinds of fungi cause fatal poisoning, most kinds producing no more than mild to severe indisposition. Absolutely fatal fungi include the **fly agaric, green and white death cap, bald paxillus, panther cap**, the **false morel**, the **orange agaric**, the **parasol mushroom** and various kinds of **clitocybe**. The poisons from these kinds of fungi lead to paralysis of the respiratory muscles after four to eight hours, and liver damage.

Dangers of poisoning from chemicals and bedding

However, not just plants, shrubs and bushes can be fatal or at least harmful to horses. Decomposing, unsuitable food, poisonous bedding materials and chemically treated fences or the walls of loose boxes too can cause life-threatening illnesses.

Poisoning by chemicals

Although in the area of stable management rather than botany, basically no poisonous paints or wood preservatives should be used: it happens again and again that poisoning arises from freshly painted wooden fences or walls of loose boxes. The most frequently used poisonous substances are lead, cresol and phenol. Lead poisoning manifests itself in tying-up of the muscles, loss of weight and staggering movements; depending on the severity of the poisoning, blindness can occur. Phenol and cresol poisoning cause an accelerated pulse, loss of appetite, colic and constipation. With timely treatment from the vet the horse can be saved, but residual impairment of health in the long term cannot be ruled out.

Bedding

Apart from straw bedding, horses must not as a general rule eat any other kinds of bedding (hemp, wood shavings or flax), as serious colic can result. Chipboard is particularly dangerous as the glues in it are toxic. Only wood shavings specifically supplied for animal management are safe, as no timber is used which has been treated with wood preservative or insecticide.

To prevent horses from eating bedding through hunger or boredom, enough dry fodder such as hay and straw must always be available.

However, far and away more dangerous is poisoning from bark litter (for paddocks or arenas), if it contains the bark of robinia (also known as false acacia) or other poisonous woods. Such barks are highly poisonous, and lead to severe illnesses and even death. When buying bark mulch, an assurance should be sought (preferably in writing) that no poisonous woods have been used.

Dangers of poisoning from decomposing food

Unsuitable storage of food frequently leads to the formation of mould or contamination from bacterial toxins. Ingesting this decomposing food is not life-threatening in all cases, but it does produce indisposition and gastritis and even severe colic. Whilst with humans mouldy and inedible food is thrown away, with horses the approach can still be that a bit of mould in the hay or silage may not be such a bad thing.

In these cases the owner of the livery stables may unfortunately be more interested in avoiding financial loss than in the health of the horses. Also, he does not have to bear the cost of the vet's bills arising from his inferior food.

In general, horses refuse inedible food, but if they are offered too little dry fodder, decomposing or mouldy hay will be eaten to satisfy hunger or the need to chew. The horse can suppress the instinctive refusal to eat food that makes it ill, if the conditions in which it finds itself are sufficiently bad.

Digestive disorders, colic, illnesses of the respiratory tract, as well as damage to the liver and kidneys, are the consequences of eating food that is decomposing, mouldy or contaminated with bacteria. The consumption of food contaminated with mould frequently causes respiratory complaints and encourages allergies. Also, particularly in the case of horses with sensitive stomachs, digestive disorders in the form of flatulence or constipation arise. In the worst case, severe distension of the stomach can occur, causing rupture of the intestine, resulting in the death of the horse. Bacilli which particularly cause illnesses lead to damage to the sensitive mucous membranes of the gut, and highly poisonous substances can enter the bloodstream, leading to circulatory failure and shock.

The use of decomposing food can lead in the long run to insidious, chronic illnesses in horses, and must be avoided for the sake of the health of the horse. A glance at the quality of the food in storage and a check of the hay should be carried out regularly as a preventive measure by the horse owner.

Salty and spicy crisps are very indigestible for horses, and can cause gastritis.

Unsuitable food in horse nutrition

The number one unsuitable food is the sugar lump, a titbit from earlier times when special horse treats were not on the market. A sugar lump now and again does not do any serious damage, but it is not typical food for a horse.

Likewise, sweets of any description are not to be fed to horses. Neither chocolate nor liquorice, biscuits nor wine gums are easily absorbed by a horse's digestive system. Sensitive horses can react with intestinal cramps, constipation or colic.

Of course highly spiced crisps and peanuts do not belong on a horse's menu either. The thin branches and twigs of known fruit trees are a healthier snack for horses.

Dried turnip tops are often given to horses in winter, but these must only be provided in a completely softened state. Unsoaked, dry scraps of food can cause dangerous blockages at the back of the throat, which can lead, without timely veterinary assistance, to the death by asphyxiation of the horse. Soaked scraps must never be given in frozen form because of an increased danger of colic and scouring. During softening, the scraps must thaw out completely. Feeding pure wheat in large quantities is life-threatening. The high proportion of gluten in wheat normally leads to compaction of the stomach contents, which can cause a fatal rupture of the stomach. The chances of recovery after a major operation in an equine hospital are usually very slight.